THE ORIGINAL

21

RULES

OF THIS HOUSE

BY GREGG & JOSH HARRIS

Noble Publishing Associates
710 NE Cleveland St. Ste 170
Gresham. Oregon 97030

Noble Publishing Associates offers its various presentations in overhead transparency kits. audio cassette tape sets and video tape seminars. as well as in live formats. Special arrangements may be made to use these materials and host these presentations for fund raising and educational purposes.

For details contact:
Director of Special Events
Noble Publishing Associates
710 NE Cleveland St. Ste 170
Gresham. Oregon 97030

Printed In Hong Kong
ISBN 0-923463-72-0

TABLE OF CONTENTS

HOW TO USE THE 21 RULES IN YOUR HOME

■ ■

Welcome to The 21 Rules of This House!

Living together with consideration for the needs and feelings of others does not happen by accident. We are either being considerate intentionally, or by default we are being *inconsiderate*. In this area of life, we can all use help.

Even when children are eager to please they often lack the information they need to behave properly. They don't always understand why they get into trouble ("What did I do?") or how to stay out of trouble. ("What do you want?") As parents, it is our responsibility to teach our children clear, simple rules that remove the uncertainty, clear up the confusion and avoid misunderstandings.

For this reason we developed *The 21 Rules of This House*. These rules define the behavior boundaries for everyone in the home. When they are used consistently, many of the frustrations of daily life are eliminated and the general atmosphere of the home is greatly improved.

The suggestions that follow will help you put *The 21 Rules* to work in your home.

Help Your Child Memorize the Rules

The first thing to do is read through the coloring book and look at the illustrations with your children. Familiarize them with all the rules. For younger children, this step should be repeated several times. Take the time to let them "study" and comment on what they see.

Next post the laminated (jelly-proofed) master list of *The 21 Rules* with magnets to your refrigerator door (or tack them to a bulletin board, whichever is most accessible and visible). Explain to any non-reading children that these are the same rules that went with the pictures in the coloring book.

Then begin a 21-week *Rule-of-the-Week Program*! In this section and the next, we offer several suggestions for things you can do to help your children learn each rule. We encourage you to spread these activities out over each week.

The first step in this program will be to post a single Rule Poster per week (or smaller increment of time if you desire) on the refrigerator or bulletin board near the master list. You may order the sequence of rules in any way you like. Target the most urgent needs in your household first. Then go back and learn the remaining rules later. They do not have to be done in numerical order.

Read the **Rule Poster** slowly to your children having each child repeat it after you. Throughout the day recite the rule to one another. At lunch, "In this house, when we make a mess, we clean it up." At dinner, "Who can recite the rule from memory for Daddy?" At nap time or bedtime, review the rule with your children. Remember: repeat, recite and review!

A reinforcing activity for each week will be coloring the corresponding illustration in the coloring book. (You have our permission to photocopy the pages so that all of your children can color the same picture at the same time. Keep the original coloring book clean and safe as your photocopy master.) Have your children recite the rule as they color the picture. Put the finished artwork up on your refrigerator or bulletin board for all to see. Let your children recite the rule for the week and describe the picture to any guests you may have in your home.

Understanding the Rules

The following exercises will further illuminate the rule of the week. As each rule is spotlighted, you will need to make certain that its meaning is clear to your children. It is especially important for the younger ones to grow in their understanding of the rule and its implications in real-life circumstances. This growth can be aided:

1. by the use of simple stories, and

2. by recalling real situations from the child's past. Both of these will help illustrate the meaning and value of each rule. They can be done at meals, during devotions or any other time the family gathers together.

Once again, remember to spread the various activities out over the week.

Simple Stories

Using your gifts as a storyteller, recount to your children situations that show a person obeying or disobeying the Rule of the Week. Familiar Bible stories reinforce many of the house rules: Jonah-Rule #1, "We obey our Lord Jesus Christ." The Prodigal Son-Rule #8, "When someone is sorry, we forgive him." and Rule #10, "When someone is happy, we rejoice with him.", and the Good Samaritan-Rule #4, "We consider one another's interests ahead of our own." Additional stories may also come from other literature.

Louisa May Alcott's classic Little Women has a gripping account of the harm that can come when Rule #8, "When someone is sorry, we forgive him." is ignored, but the best stories will usually come from your own experiences. We all

have stories to tell that clearly communicate not only the meaning of each rule but the subsequent blessing or burden created by the positive or negative response to it. It can be as small as how the picnic lunch was considerably less enjoyable because Susan didn't obey Rule #15, "When we open something, we close it." (The potato chips were stale!) Or it can be as dramatic as how eighty-year-old grandma fell because someone broke Rule #17, "When we take something out, we put it away."

Recalling Past Experiences

Your children will be more active participants in the recalling of past occasions when they have disobeyed the Rule of the Week. Ask them to explain what they would have done differently if they had known this rule. At this point, when it is possible, the children can act out the same situation again with the proper behavior replac-

ing their misbehavior. This gives them practice in doing the right thing. We did this with our twins when one lost his temper and raised his voice in anger to the other. We recreated the scene and let them practice obeying Rule #5, "In this house, we speak quietly and respectfully with one another." It really worked!

basis of what had been decided beforehand.

How to Administer Proper Discipline

Many parents use the following three steps as an approach to discipline:

cy to be harsh or lenient with the scriptural teachings of God's mercies which are new every morning and the need for children to experience the reality of God's justice as they reap what they have sown.

Learning to Obey the Rules

Obedience to the rules will come only through a process of training that includes appropriate and very predictable consequences to disobedience. We must establish a consistent approach, enforcing the rules as needed. The first step in administering discipline is to discuss with your children the consequences for disobeying any of the rules before any disobedience actually occurs. They will usually agree to fair and reasonable discipline. Get their suggestions; then YOU decide what is appropriate. By doing this, you will be able to respond to any offense clearly on the

1. First violation of a new rule–a gentle reminder

2. Second violation of the same rule–a stern rebuke

3. Third violation of the same rule–a spanking or the loss of a privilege

Most Christian child training experts agree that spanking is appropriate only when a child is in open defiance to what he knows his parents have told him to do. Even then, spanking should never be done in anger. When deep sorrow and repentance has been demonstrated, corporal punishment may be called off. Each situation and child must be dealt with individually. Balance your own tenden-

Additional Considerations

An attentive parent can often ward off wrong behavior before it starts. When you hear your child begin to raise his voice in anger, simply say, "In this house, we speak quietly and respectfully with one another." When an art project is finished and the children are about to run out the door to ride bikes, "In this house, when we make a mess we clean it up." Our children are so accustomed to this that after I have said, "In this house…", they pipe in with the appropriate rule. This is great. It shows that they are very well-trained but far from being perfect!

Patience on the part of parents is needed in this child training process. It is at least a good twenty-year commitment. The longer the old patterns have been in force, the longer it will take for the good habits to be established. (Ah, there's another lesson in sowing and reaping.) But remember, prayer and persistence do produce results!

Closing Thoughts

We hope that you will enjoy using *The 21 Rules of This House* in your home. They are intended to help you accomplish an important goal—that of creating a quiet and peaceable atmosphere in your home. This can be done only by training family members to live considerately with one another.

Remember that the giving of the 10 Commandments to Moses did not bring about instant righteousness in the people of Israel. Instead, when faced honestly, they exposed the sinfulness of mankind. That was part of God's intention. He wanted the people to turn to Him for forgiveness and help.

In a similar way, *The 21 Rules of This House* will expose weaknesses in your family as well. Even mom and dad may struggle to comply with some rules. This should cause us to turn to God for His forgiveness and help. The Holy Spirit is working in our lives. That is why we have a great hope as we commit ourselves to live lovingly with one another.

Some religious leaders used God's law to condemn and manipulate their fellowman. They strained at gnats and swallowed camels. Rather than drawing people closer together, they used God's law to distance themselves from others. Jesus criticized this abuse of God's Word. He knew the heart of God's law.

The 21 Rules are never intended to create distance between you and your children. They are not created for your convenience in controlling your children. The purpose of the rules is to reduce strife and bring family members into closer relationships with Christ and with one another. They are to serve as a means of training ourselves as well as our children to behave properly. Our goal is to more effectively show God's love to each other and the unbelieving world. If we do it right, outsiders will marvel and say, "Behold, how they love one another." That is the heart of *The 21 Rules of This House.*

~ *The Harris Family*

1. We obey our Lord Jesus Christ.

2. We love, honor and pray for one another.

3. We tell the truth.

4. We consider one another's interests ahead of our own.

5. We speak quietly and respectfully with one another.

6. We do not hurt one another with unkind words or deeds.

7. When someone needs correction, we correct him in love.

8. When someone is sorry, we forgive him.

9. When someone is sad, we comfort him.

10. When someone is happy, we rejoice with him.

11. When we have something nice to share, we share it.

12. When we have work to do, we do it without complaining.

13. We take good care of everything God has given us.

14. We do not create unnecessary work for others.

16. When we turn something on, we turn it off.

18. When we make a mess, we clean it up.

19. When we do not know what to do, we ask.

20. When we go out, we act just as if we were in this house.

21. When we disobey or forget any of the 21 Rules of this House, we accept discipline and instruction.

1.
We obey our Lord
Jesus Christ.

2.

We love, honor and
pray for one another.

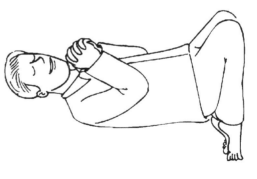

3.

We tell the truth.

4.

We consider one another's interests ahead of our own.

5.

We speak quietly
and respectfully with
one another.

6.

We do not hurt one another with unkind words or deeds.

7.

When someone needs correction, we correct him in love.

8.

When someone is
sorry, we forgive him.

9.
When someone
is sad, we
comfort him.

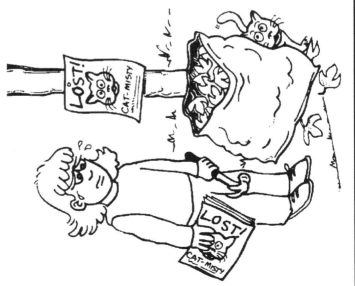

10.

When someone is happy, we rejoice with him.

11.
When we have
something nice to
share, we
share it.

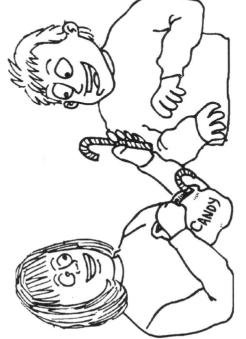

12.

When we have work
to do, we do it
without
complaining.

13.

We take good care
of everything
God has
given us.

14.

We do not create
unnecessary work
for others.

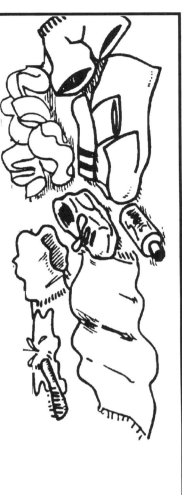

15.

When we open
something,
we close it.

16.

When we turn
something on,
we turn it off.

17.

When we take

something out,

we put

it away.

18.

When we make a
mess, we
clean it up.

19.
When we do not
know what
to do,
we ask.

20.

When we go out,

we act just as

if we were

in this house.

21.

When we disobey or forget any of The 21 Rules of this House, we accept discipline and instruction.

Uncommon Courtesy

Let's face up to the fact that "common courtesy" isn't as common as it used to be! Proper etiquette is practically extinct. Uncommon Courtesy for Kids teaches children 56 ways to be considerate of others. It will help your children understand what to do and what not to do in eleven different situations. This kit covers everything from meal times to going to church. Includes a laminated list of all 56 rules, a reproducible coloring book, and individual posters for each rule. For ages 3 and up.
Item #1042..........$13⁹⁵

Rules For Young Friends

Do you feel overrun by your child's playmates? This valuable resource provides 11 simple rules for friendships. Rules For Young Friends is a coloring book curriculum that will help you teach your child to be a good host and a good guest. In addition to family house rules, this set includes rules for loyalty towards family members, borrowing and loaning toys, friends who interrupt chores and much more. This training kit has worked for thousands of families, and it can work for you.
Item #1036..........$12⁹⁵

The Choreganizer

Overwhelmed by household chores at your house? *The Choreganizer* to the rescue! This valuable tool helps you: **1) Identify all the household chores that need to be done** (with 60 colorful chore cards). **2) Assign them to your children** (on individualized chore charts) and **3) Monitor completion on a daily basis.** Visually appealing and fun to use, it also offers its unique **Chore Store, Mom Money** and **Dad Dollars** giving your children tangible goals to work toward and a way for you to say "thanks for helping."
Item #1725..........$16⁹⁵

WILL YOUR CHILD BE A FOLLOWER OR A LEADER?

Dr. Jeff Myers has found that people who communicate well are chosen to be leaders. His new book *From Playpen to Podium* shows you how to improve your child's communication skills through reading, writing and thinking skills. It also enhances their comfort in social situations, helps them resist negative peer influences, and develops leadership skills. Now you can easily give your children the communication advantage.

Item #1799 ....$12⁹⁵